THE JEWISH FAMILY ALBUM

FRANZ HUBMANN

THE JEWISH FAMILY ALBUM

THE LIFE OF A PEOPLE
IN PHOTOGRAPHS

Text by
MIRIAM AND LIONEL KOCHAN

LITTLE, BROWN AND COMPANY
BOSTON   TORONTO

LIBRARY OF CONGRESS CATALOG CARD NO. 74-19873

FIRST AMERICAN EDITION

Published simultaneously in Canada
by Little, Brown & Company (Canada) Limited

PRINTED IN AUSTRIA

CONTENTS

INTRODUCTION

For nearly two thousand years the Jews have wandered landless over the face of the earth. Between 70 C.E. and 1948 they settled first in this country, then in that. They were driven from one land to another. They left one seemingly permanent home to find another of equal promise.

The wandering Jew is an eternal image. In this book, however, the camera has caught the Jew at moments of settlement and recorded him for eternity. It is amazing how settled he seems. It appears unbelievable that the elderly Polish Jews taking a summer stroll in the countryside of Galicia have not an age-old past stretching behind them, an interminable future ahead. The Viennese aristocrats lounging nonchalantly in their elegant salons seem bred of hundreds of years of power and affluence, destined to rule from their fauteuils for generations to come.

This chameleon-like quality of the Jew, his power to assume in record time the characteristics of the people amongst whom circumstances ordain that he live, makes it difficult to think of all the varied personality-types portrayed in these pages as members of one and the same family. What can relate the bearded Polish street-cleaner photographed in 1914 to Sarah Bernhardt, the lovely darling of the Paris stage, or either of them to Bernard Baruch, the illustrious economic adviser to successive American presidents from Theodore Roosevelt to John F. Kennedy? What, in fact, brings them all together in the pages of history?

Basically, the answer is, of course, the religion shared over the course of the millennia, but the Jews, as their history has shown, are considerably more than a religious group. Yet they cannot be regarded as a nation either. Anthropologists have rejected the notion of 'a Jewish race'. Sociology offers a solution in the cumbersome description of a 'socio-religious group'. How much happier to consider them a family, tracing its genealogy back to Abraham, to whom the existence of the one God was first revealed and who began the pilgrimage in obedience to His will. They are a family whose history has scattered them over the world but whose bonds of faith have continued to unite them through the vicissitudes of fortune.

The pattern is repeated more obviously on the smaller scale of the individual Jewish community. Here, an age-old tradition of self-help still exists to this day. Every member feels a shared responsibility for the well-being of the whole.

It is Judaism, too, which is a dominant factor in keeping alive the sense of shared history—another of the strands which, together with the shared responsibility, binds together the dispersed and disparate family. Each Jew is instructed to identify himself with the same past. For example the head of the household is commanded, when he reads, at the festival of the Passover, the story of the Exodus of the Jews from Egypt each year, to relate the events as if they happened to himself and not as though some vague and distant ancestors were involved. So each member of the great Jewish family feels this sense of a joint past. The history of the Bible is the history of every Jew today. In the more recent times portrayed in this book, the gnarled Russian peasant is every Jew's grandfather. The six million Jews who perished in the Nazi holocaust are mourned as the loss of a relative. The land of Israel today is every Jew's spiritual homeland.

'Family' is in any case a peculiarly evocative word in its application to the Jews. Perhaps because almost everywhere they live as minority groups transplanted onto alien soil or because of their religious ritual which prescribes so many ceremonies to be carried out inside the home, his own individual family is of immense importance to the individual Jew. A very tight-knit family relationship grows up around the Kiddush service recited over the bread and wine by the father on the eve of the Sabbath on Friday night, or around the menorah, the eight-branched candelabrum, lit in the home during the festival of Chanukah, to celebrate the Jews' victory over the Greeks.

It is normal to date the dispersion of the Jewish people from the ninth of the Jewish month of Av in the year 70 C.E., the day when the Roman armies broke into the Temple in Jerusalem. During the siege of the city which preceded it, 600,000 Jews died. In the months which followed, almost the same number were taken as prisoners to Rome, where Jews had in fact been settled since the second century B.C.E.

When Jerusalem fell to the Romans in 70 C.E., there were already many Jewish settlements scattered over the world in which the Jews could seek refuge. From this point in time begins their existence as a homeless family dispersed amongst the nations . . . It is from this moment that attention swings sharply round to focus on the Western World, on Europe.

Nothing changed the destiny of the scattered Jewish family in Europe more than the spread in the West of the new monotheistic religion, Christianity. The image of the Jew which then emerged was born of the contemporary teachings of the Christian Church, namely that the Jews had killed Christ. They were guilty of the crime of deicide. Their only hope of salvation lay in renouncing their own religion and converting to Christianity.

A more drastic stage in the campaign to exclude Jews from Christian society came with the institution of the ghetto. In many of the Italian and German states from the sixteenth century onward they were only permitted to live in a specific district of a town, closed by locked gates at night and characterised by its high, dark, over-populated houses and narrow streets, teeming with active, over-crowded Jewish life. The first compulsory ghetto seems to have been established in Breslau in the thirteenth century. The system of restricting areas in which the Jews could live was in a sense repeated in the Russian Pale of Settlement which persisted until the February Revolution of 1917.

Gradually the Jews found new homes. Slowly the countries which had expelled them re-opened their doors; England, for example, re-admitted them under Oliver Cromwell in 1656. But the ghetto walls, whether built of stone or of social prejudice, remained high. The restrictions governing their activities continued in force. Their position outside the bounds of society was relatively unchanged. Many years were to pass before the ghetto walls of Europe cracked, crumbled and collapsed.

The intellectual wind that swept over Europe at the end of the eighteenth century, which blew down the mighty monarchy of France, completely changed, first the image, then the actual status of the Jew. From the ideas contained in the writings of the Englishman John Locke and the Frenchmen Jean-Jacques

Rousseau and Charles de Secondat Baron de Montesquieu, the theory of the equality of all men gained ground.

The new ideas were embodied in the first constitution of America. In rolling phrases it proclaimed the political equality of every citizen of the new democracy regardless of religion. Here at least the Jew was at last politically on a par with the people amongst whom he lived. The Reverend Gershom Mendez Seixas, Cantor of the Mikveh Israel congregation, marched between two Christian ministers at the head of a procession of five thousand citizens through the streets of Philadelphia to celebrate the ratification of the new constitution in 1788.

The Old World too, with centuries of tradition behind it, was not slow to bend in its turn to the wind of the Enlightenment. As early as 1781, Joseph II, Holy Roman Emperor and an enlightened despot, published a Patent of Toleration which abolished the yellow badge that Jews had to wear and also the body tax they had to pay merely for the right to exist. Joseph also enlarged Jewish educational and occupational opportunities. On the other hand, he severely restricted the number of Jews who might live in Vienna and Lower Austria. Joseph issued similar Patents for the other areas of the Habsburg dominions where Jews lived—Bohemia, Moravia, Silesia and Galicia.

In France, the very heart of the Enlightenment, the National Assembly set up after the revolution in 1789 made haste to give practical expression to similar sentiments. On 28 September 1791, the Jews were declared equal with all men as free citizens of France.

The movement to free the Jew from his physical fetters of inequality did not come only from the Christian world outside the ghetto. The Jews themselves had already been battering from within for a long time.

A second 'revolution' also played a part in changing the position of the Jew in Western society. This was the industrial revolution.

The phenomenon of Jewish capital financing the transition to the capitalist economy was nowhere more clearly marked than in Germany—though it is important that this should not be exaggerated. None the less, the first iron foundry and smelting plant was built in Silesia in the 1840s by Moritz Friedländer, Simon Levy and David Löwenfeld. The Caro brothers and Moritz Friedländer established the coke industry there. Bethel Henry Strousberg was the great railway builder of northern Germany. Albert Ballin (pictured on page 224) created the Hamburg—America shipping line; Emil Rathenau organised the Allgemeine Elektrizitäts-Gesellschaft, which supplied all Germany with electric power; and some of the biggest department stores in the country were founded and owned by Jews. And of course, there was always banking. Led by the incomparable Rothschilds, the Jews came right to the fore, flourished and grew rich. When Mayer Amschel Rothschild of Frankfurt died in 1812, he left behind him a powerful banking house and five sons to carry on branch establishments throughout Europe.

The pattern was repeated in every major European country: the Rothschilds at the centre of the galaxy, surrounded by lesser though still brilliant stars. In France, the brothers Isaac and Emile Péreire founded the Crédit Mobilier and, with their cousin Olinde Rodrigues built the first railway in France in 1835. In England, that great philanthropist Sir Moses Montefiore supplied the first lighting to London's streets through his Imperial Continental Gas Association. In the United States, the itinerant pedlar Lazarus Straus was the founder of two of the country's greatest stores, Macy's in New York, Abraham and Straus in Brooklyn.

Money brought power. The Rothschilds were generally regarded as some of the most powerful men in Europe, able to mediate in questions of peace and war, life and death. The promise of a loan here, the calling in of a debt there could tip the fragile balance between a European conflagration and an honorable solution to a conflict. Money also brought luxury, high living, beautiful homes and elegant appurtenances.

Money, however, could not always buy the social equality that some Jews now hungered for. Their appetites had been whetted. They were wealthy. Now they wanted the social recognition and distinction that were appropriate to their newly acquired status. In the great European capitals wealthy Jewish women with social and intellectual aspirations held salons and opened the doors of their magnificent homes to the great of the world. The salon conducted in Vienna by Fanny von Arnstein (the daughter of the successful Berlin banker Itzig) drew international leaders of all shades of opinion attending the Congress of Vienna in 1814–15. It was fashionable to be seen there and guests ranged from emperors to church dignitaries. Similar, equally famous, salons were held in Berlin by hostesses such as Rahel Varnhagen von Ense, Henriette Herz and Moses Mendelssohn's daughter Dorothea. Here again, the famous names of contemporary society gathered in the house of the Jew.

Many of these women had bought 'their entrance ticket to European culture', to quote Heinrich Heine, the great German-Jewish poet, by converting to Christianity. The motive which drove them to renounce their religion was a prominent feature of the Jewish world of their day. It was a symptom of the desire for social acceptance by the Christian world which all the money in the world did not seem able to procure. It is estimated, possibly inaccurately, that at least half of Berlin's Jewish community was voluntarily baptised in the mid-nineteenth century.

Because they regarded themselves as French, German, Austrian citizens, no uniform political beliefs are found amongst the Jews of the various countries. In fact, they were and are found on every side of the political fence. In Germany for example, birthplace of the baptised Jew Karl Marx and of Ferdinand Lassalle who organised the General German Workers' Association in 1863, the principal theorist of the Christian Constitutional State was the Jewish convert to Christianity Friedrich Julius Stahl. In Austria, two of the principal revolutionary leaders in Vienna were Jews; Adolph Fischhof, a doctor by profession, was chairman of the Committee of Security formed in 1848 and Ignaz Kuranda, a political journalist from Prague, was first president of the new parliament in 1848. In England, Jews entered the House of Commons when the oath 'on the true faith of a Christian' ceased to become a condition of entry in 1857. Lionel de Rothschild who had first been elected in 1847 was readily admitted in 1858.

The Jews of Eastern Europe are different. Their difference leaps at us from these pages. They seem to spring from a different world, a different century. With their horse-drawn carts, their archaic garb, their poverty and their simplicity, industrialisation and modern civilisation seem to have passed them by.

What is it that has made the East European Jew different from his Western relations? Why, in his case, has the course of history taken a different turn?

Unlike other European countries, during the medieval period, the condition of the Jews, of Poland was relatively tolerable. And it was in Poland that the largest Jewish communities were to be found during this period, their numbers constantly swollen by the flight eastwards as the massacring forces of the Crusades swept over the West. The tone of royal protection of this growing body was set by a series of enactments which appeared around 1264 in the reign of King Boleslaw the Pious. Declaring his intention to give equal protection to Jew and Christian, the king forbade desecration of or physical injury to synagogues, Jewish schools and cemeteries. Full protection was accorded to all Jews and their possessions. They were free to travel everywhere without molestation, and if they were attacked, it was the duty of every Christian to defend them. Ritual murder charges against Jews were pronounced to be false and slanderous and were forbidden. If, however, a Christian persisted in such an allegation, he had to produce six witnesses, three of whom were Jews. These benign provisions were extended by a later Polish monarch, Casimir the Great (1333–70) who permitted Jews to rent not only estates but whole villages from feudal landowners.

This happy state of affairs could not last. The anti-Jewish feeling, already noted, took shape in the imposition of restrictions on Jewish trade. One consequence was that Jews turned in large numbers to the considerably more stable occupations offered by handicrafts. In no other European country were there so many Jewish artisans as in Poland in the sixteenth century. Their numbers were so great that in cases when the Christian guilds excluded them, they were able to form guilds of their own.

By the sixteenth century, another interesting and unparalleled phenomenon had emerged in the area. The mass arrival of Jews from Germany and Bohemia fleeing from the Crusaders in the middle of the fourteenth century led to the birth of a totally individual Yiddish-speaking culture, an amalgam of the German culture brought in by the new immigrants and the Slavic culture of the long-standing inhabitants. By the sixteenth century, this Yiddish culture had crystallised, flowered and expanded. It was one of the most significant features of East European Jewry, perhaps the most important factor which differentiated it from Jewries elsewhere.

It was another feature which separated the Jews of Poland from the population around them. Already they lay at the margins of feudal society, and they were differentiated by their religion. Now the barrier was strengthened by the difference in cultures. The state added its might to the creation of a separate Jewish world by encouraging the *kahal*, the Jewish communal organisation, governed by a board of elders elected annually by the community, to become the administrative organ of Jewish self-government. It had the great advantage in their eyes of being a highly efficient tax-collecting agency responsible for preserving peace in the ghetto and also for carrying out the orders of the state.

In actuality, the *kahal* became something very much more than an organ of governmental control. It became the very hub of Jewish communal life, of that rich, warm Yiddish culture, pervaded by the embracing mantle of the shared religion and the shared way of life. It provided religious and communal institutions, cared for the poor, the sick, the victims of disasters, orphans and widows. It dispensed justice through its own *beth din* (law court), supervised the religious education of the young (always considered of prime importance) and arranged the burial of the dead. It regulated the conduct of businessmen and artisans, and generally built up a group life which more than compensated for the Jew's isolation from the Christian world he lived in.

It was this isolation, sheltered under the warm wings of the *kahal*, which was responsible for the Jew's remoteness from contemporary society. In the nineteenth century, even the twentieth, he is seen in the pages of this book as wearing garments which were fashionable in Russia and Poland in medieval times. Centuries after the Russians and Poles had discarded them in favour of Western garb, Polish and Russian Jews were still wearing the long caftan and fur trimmed hat. Today, they are still worn by the mystical sect of Hasidic Jews.

It is from this period that the earliest examples of the very typical wooden synagogues of Poland date —though this is not to say that earlier models did not exist; wood is a highly perishable material. Sometimes built with pagoda-type roofs, later (by the end of the eighteenth century) with saddle and mansard roofs, their exquisite decoration provided wonderful opportunities for Jewish artisans of every type to exercise their skill and demonstrate their devotion.

The legacy of the golden age of the *kahal*, of the rich Jewish education and communal life it provided remained, but as the seventeenth century advanced disaster followed disaster. The Jews were the victims of violence in the Cossack revolt of 1648, in the Polish massacres of 1654 and in the peasant revolts of the first half of the eighteenth century. Towards the end of that fateful century, when by the three partitions of Poland, most of Polish Jewry had become the subjects of the Russian crown, a movement began to isolate the Jews from the general population even further. This passed into the law of the land in 1804 when the Pale of Settlement was set up in the western provinces of the Russian Empire and Jews were forbidden to live outside already established communities. Other restrictions followed: the Tsar Alexander I forbade Jews to continue as tavern and inn-keepers in villages in some areas and ordered that in future they live only in towns; Nicholas I, his successor, extended this policy to hitherto unaffected areas. Displaced Jews wandered wretchedly into the small towns of the Pale. No longer were there jobs enough to keep the once-active wheels of their economy turning; money enough to care for the sick, the needy and the old. Nor yet was there the money to pay the ever-onerous taxes to the state. The prosperous *kahals* were reduced to unprecedented poverty. But their cultural warmth, their religious bonds remained. They are perpetuated for us in the works of Sholem Aleichem. The recent production of *Fiddler on the Roof* has revived their totally individual atmosphere for all the world to see.

The blows continued to fall. In 1827, Nicholas I, in an attempt to turn the Jews into good Russian citizens (a governmental dream which was periodically revived), instituted compulsory military service for a period of twenty-five years for a set number of Jewish recruits to be delivered by each *kahal*. Painfully, searingly, the communities handed over their boys between the ages of twelve and eighteen to the army. Economic problems also continued to accumulate. Alexander II's liberation of the serfs in 1861 freed thousands upon thousands of able-bodied men to compete with Jews in the employment market. The industrial revolution which came late in Russia, robbed many Jewish craftsmen of their source of income. In 1881, with the accession of Alexander III to the Russian throne, the pogroms, a source of terror in the past, gathered strength and spread. Jewish houses and shops were destroyed, Jewish property looted, women violated, Jews killed. Not a Jew in Russia could feel secure that next time the scourge would not strike *him*.

Hopelessly, helplessly, the Eastern European Jews realised that there no longer existed for them a future in the lands of their birth. It is from this point, that their large-scale emigration westwards begins . . .

The main goal of the thousands upon thousands of Eastern European Jews planning to leave their inhospitable homelands was the United States of America. It shone like a beacon in the dark. It was a symbol of the liberty, equality and security they lacked. It seemed to offer the abundance of opportunity and the scope for improvement they had always dreamed of.

No accurate statistics are available before 1899, but it is estimated that of the 700,000 Jews who fled from Russia and Poland between 1884 and 1903, 500,000 went to America. After 1903 and a further round of Russian pogroms, numbers increased. In 1903, 77,544 Eastern European Jews entered the United States; in 1904, 92,388; in 1905, 125,234; and in 1907, 114, 932.

The larger proportion of all these immigrants, most of them almost penniless, all of them disoriented and bewildered, lived for a period at least in the Lower East Side area of New York. (It had its equivalent on a considerably smaller scale in most of the European capitals, for example, Whitechapel in the East End of London.) Here, they found a ready-made Jewish community already in existence. Even by the time of the American Civil War, this once-fashionable district had become the Jewish quarter of the city. The tall, dark, narrow tenements were already crowded with German and Hungarian immigrant families. They filled to bursting as the fast-flowing stream of Eastern Europeans rushed in.

Living together in this over-crowded proximity, they tried in a way to re-create the world of the ghetto.

As they had done there, they formed every type of mutual aid society. Desperately poor themselves, they formed societies to care for their poor, groups for study, groups to arrange for the education of their children, groups for worship. Literally hundreds of small synagogues or 'stiebls' sprang up for prayer.

Sheltered within the warmth of this poor but closely-knit entity, the Jew had still to earn a livelihood. For this he was, in many cases, particularly unsuited. There was, of course, the language problem. There was also the fact that many of these East European Jews had been small-scale traders in their homelands and, without capital or skills, were totally unfitted to find easy employment in their new milieu. But they took up the challenge. One opening at least seemed within the realm of possibility: they took to the streets as pedlars. Pushing barrows, carrying baskets, packs on their backs, they thronged the East Side, offering for sale every type of food, dry goods or knick-knacks. They needed little capital to engage in such a trade and though the profits they brought home were small, turnover at least was rapid. Gradually, from these small profits, some of them succeeded in saving enough to open small food shops of their own, to move out of the East Side. Some even became the founders of the massive department stores of present-day America.

Those who had been fortunate enough to possess some skill when they arrived found employment more easily. Many thousands had indeed been engaged in sewing trades in Eastern Europe. Now they were sucked into the American clothing industry, which had been initiated in the 1870s by Hungarian and German Jews. Demand was insatiable for this cheap labour which was so easy to exploit. Unable to speak the language of the country, too insecure in these early days to assert themselves, they provided easy and plentiful man (and woman) power for the 'sweatshops', where, in abominable conditions of bad light and overcrowding, they worked with their needles for between twelve and eighteen hours a day for six days a week, in an effort to feed and clothe themselves and their families, to build up the new life. The 1900 census shows that 53 per cent of all male Eastern European workers in America and 72 per cent of all female were engaged in the sewing trades.

Yet amidst this poverty, amidst this life of hardship and unremitting toil, a warm Yiddish-speaking culture thrived anew on American soil. By 1900, six large, all-Yiddish daily papers circulated in New York, as well as innumerable periodicals. A Yiddish-speaking intelligentsia had grown up; there were Yiddish authors and Yiddish poets; and above all, there was a Yiddish theatre to which all thronged.

The world of the assimilated Jews in Europe was built on less firm foundations. There were constant reminders for those prepared to listen that the security they had created was illusory. Though protected by a fair degree of political equality, and often cushioned by their wealth and social status, they could not help but be aware to some extent of the under-current of anti-Jewish feeling which never died. And this feeling, in the same way as it showed that the world around still saw the Jew in the respected citizen, also served as a constant reminder to the Jew that beyond his identity as a respected citizen he was a member of the great Jewish family.

Events moved rapidly now towards the climax which was to turn the spotlight of hate and destruction onto the whole family.

By the end of the First World War in 1918, the scene was fully set for the cataclysm. All the necessary elements were in place. The racial theory of Aryan superiority and Jewish inferiority had been authoritatively formulated and had been accepted by many scientists, anthropologists and politicians. The tendency to place the blame for all the ills of mankind on the Jews was ready to be exploited. Organisations were in existence to ensure that this trend was utilised to serve any purpose it was required for: in Russia, the Tsar's Black Hundreds; in France the Anti-Dreyfusards; and in Germany, a secret terrorist organisation, the Fehme.

Germany, hearth of Aryanism, beset with disillusion and humiliation after the defeat of the war, was an inevitable breeding ground for the movement. Her sense of pride in her national destiny grievously offended, burdened with a heavy load of war reparations, she was urgently in need of a scapegoat to carry the blame, a strong policy to unite and give back hope to a disappointed people, and a charismatic leader to restore their national pride. All three factors materialised. Adolf Hitler, at the head of the National Socialist Party, produced a policy of world conquest by a Germany cleansed of all external racial elements (which encompassed the taint of Jewish blood). He offered an attractive future based on Aryan domination of the world.

The National Socialist Party, right from the beginning, made no secret of its attitude to the Jews. 'No Jew can be considered a fellow-countryman', its programme proudly proclaimed. A pamphlet published in the 1920s and entitled 'Hitler's Official Programme', declared 'Anti-Semitism is, in a sense, the emotional foundation of our movement'. On 30 January 1933, Hitler and the National Socialist Party assumed supreme power in Germany. Hitler's official programme became the policy of the Third Reich.

The process began with the moral and material destruction of the Jews in Germany, and their elimination from every area of national culture and economic activity. Jews were forbidden to frequent public places or to have social contacts with non-Jews. An official boycott of Jewish businesses was imposed in April 1933. Two years later to the month, Jewish children were banned from German schools. The privileges of equality, painfully acquired in the century since emancipation, disappeared within a couple of years. The logical conclusion came in September 1935 when Hitler's Nuremberg racial laws pronounced that anyone who was more than a quarter Jewish in descent was not to be regarded as a German nor entitled to German citizenship. The same laws re-instituted the ghetto, subjected the Jews to forced labour, deprived them of their property and professions, and placed them under the direct jurisdiction of the *Sicherheitsdienst*, later combined with the Gestapo, the secret state police. The following year, a Race Bureau was set up. At one fell swoop, the whole concept of Jewish emancipation had been destroyed and the Jew had returned to his medieval position outside society as a degraded being.

It might have been supposed that in these circumstances, the Jews of Germany would have followed the path of exile which their forefathers had taken on so many occasions in the past and embarked en masse to join their more happily situated brethren in America, Palestine or Britain. Many, of course, read the signs correctly, and left the country in good time. An amazingly large number remained too long, cushioned in their wealth and their security, unable to believe that this could happen to them. They were Germans, they had lived in Germany for many generations. They had fought for Germany in the First World War if not in the Franco-Prussian War of 1870. When the Nuremberg Laws were promulgated, leading German Jews inserted an advertisement in the press. The substance of their announcement was contained in the statement 'We regard ourselves, along with the overwhelming majority of German Jews, as members of the German, not of the Jewish people'.

The holocaust which ensued—the concentration camps, deportations, the gas chambers, the torture, starvation and cruelty, the experiments on living human beings—has been described too often and is too soul-searing to bear repetition. Never before had the world witnessed murder on such a massive and deliberate scale. Never before had an attempt been made to exterminate a whole people, a whole family. When the victorious Allied armies of liberation came upon the concentration camps in 1945, the horrors they disclosed devastated the free world. The shattered remnants of humanity, the survivors that crawled out of the camps to greet them, were virtually all that remained of the proud assimilated members of the

Jewish family in Berlin, Vienna, Prague... Regardless of their wealth, their achievement, their assimilation, even of their conversion to Christianity, they lay dead, buried in the mass graves of Hitler's Germany.

The centre of family life has, in fact, returned to the East. Small communities remain in old Europe. A large, prosperous and influential branch flourishes in the United States of America. But the emotions of all, the family feeling, are concentrated on the family home in the land of Israel. For the homeless wanderers have, after nearly two millennia, a home at last.

There is, of course, nothing new about the Jew's emotional involvement with the land of Israel. It has, since Abraham, been the promised land into which God led the Children of Israel after their slavery in Egypt. The Jew throughout the dispersion, and still today, prays with his face towards Jerusalem, the holy city, regards existence in the diaspora as a time of exile, and yearns in almost all his prayers for the coming of the Messiah, which will bring about the ingathering of the peoples in their homeland.

What was new was the attempt to force the issue, the decision not to wait for the Messiah but to create by human effort a homeland for the homeless people in the small country of Palestine, under Turkish rule and containing only some 20,000 pious Jews who had gone there to die or to devote themselves to prayer. Today, there seems nothing revolutionary in this concept. It burst upon the early champions of the doctrine of Zionism like a revelation.

It was born of religious persecution, and, in the latter half of the nineteenth century when its first physical manifestations appeared, the hearth of such persecution was situated in the poverty and penury of Eastern Europe.

Settlements were not slow to be formed. Between 1882 and 1903, under the impetus of the Hovevei Zion (Lovers of Zion) movement, inspired by Rabbi Samuel Mohilever (1824–1898), some 25,000 settlers arrived in Palestine from Russia and Rumania. The first branch of our Jewish family had staked its positive claim to the soil of the homeland. Spiritually, they were secure from religious persecution but physically, life was hard. In the face of the problems posed by the difficult soil and different climate of the new land, by disease and by the hostility both of the Turkish authorities and the older Jewish inhabitants, the first East European settlements in Palestine were founded: Rehovoth, Rosh Pinah, Rishon le Zion, Zichron Yaakov...

Rabbi Mohilever's Eastern European Hovevei Zion Group was the first Zionist organisation history has recorded, but the credit for being the founder of world Zionism must indisputably go to a Western European 'assimilated' Jew, Theodor Herzl. Here again, the stimulus came from religious persecution, in this instance the Dreyfus case. As a young Viennese journalist, Herzl found himself sent to Paris to report Dreyfus's trial. He was so moved and disturbed by the victimisation of the French Jewish soldier that on his return home, he sat down and wrote *Der Judenstaat (The Jewish State)*, a programme of political Zionism based not on land colonisation but on the acquisition of a State, recognised politically by the great international powers.

He, too, applied unsuccessfully to the wealthy assimilated Jews for support, and also to rulers and political leaders, before he devoted the remainder of his life to creating a mass movement amongst the main body of the Jews of the world. Membership in the organisation he initiated, the World Zionist Organisation, was made particularly easy for every member of the family, however great his poverty. All that was in fact demanded was adherence to the Society's programme and the annual payment of one shekel towards its implementation. This programme had been drawn up at the first Zionist Congress which Herzl called in Basle in 1897. 'The aim of Zionism', it proclaimed, 'is to create for the Jewish people a home in Palestine secured by public law.'

As the popularity of the doctrine of Zionism boomed, immigration to Palestine increased. Between 1904 and 1914, the second 'aliyah' (immigration) took place, bringing a new type of settler to the land and a strong wind of the ideology which has shaped and continues to shape its destiny. The new immigrants were still from Eastern Europe, this time from Russia and Poland, but they were to a large extent students and intellectuals, mainly belonging to a left-wing Zionist group, Poale Zion. They were filled with the desire to return to the land, their land, to work its soil with their own hands, to break away from the diaspora tradition of trade and engage in positive productive activity. A decision was taken at an open air meeting to build the town of Tel Aviv on a stretch of sand dunes outside the Arab city of Jaffa.

Then came the First World War and the embryo Jewish state assumed the role of a tool in the Middle Eastern policies of the Great Powers. None the less, when, in 1917, Lord Balfour, the British Foreign Secretary, wrote his famous letter to Lord Rothschild, it marked a historic moment in the history of the Jewish homeland. 'His Majesty's Government', he wrote, 'view with favour the establishment in Palestine of a national home for the Jewish people and will use their best endeavours to facilitate the achievement of this object.' Despite the varying interpretations placed upon some sentences in the declaration, Jewish life in Palestine went forward on a wave of optimism under the British Mandate which replaced Turkish rule after the war. The Mandate in theory recognised 'the historical connection of the Jewish people with Palestine' and 'the grounds for reconstituting their National Home in that country'. It took responsibility 'for placing the country under such political, administrative and economic conditions as will secure the establishment of the Jewish National Home'. The Jewish population of Palestine, halved during the First World War (from an unofficially estimated 100,000 to approximately 50,000), was swelled by some 60,000 new European settlers between 1918 and 1925, and a further 84,000 in the period from 1925 to 1935. The towns boomed: Tel Aviv and Haifa grew into small cities. New businesses were opened, old ones thrived. Small factories worked furiously. Construction works covered the land; and a hundred new agricultural settlements were founded in the eighteen years which followed the Balfour Declaration.

In the 1930s the character of the immigration changed. Many of the newcomers who arrived at the time came from the assimilated branches of the family, fleeing now from Hitler's Germany. They were highly skilled, highly educated professional people. Their advent gave a tremendous stimulus to the cultural and economic life of the homeland.

But this story of almost constant uninhibited growth and expansion was not to continue undisturbed. The conflict between Jew and Arab for possession of the country had grown throughout the period of the Jewish re-settlement, exploding from time to time into uncontrollable violence and forcing the Jewish colonists to form their own defence forces, the well-known Haganah. Already in 1937, the British Peel Commission had declared the Mandate unworkable and had recommended the partition of the country between Jew and Arab. In 1939, the British White Paper, with an eye to Arab support in the international conflict ahead, took the cruel measure of curbing Jewish immigration into Palestine — at the very moment when the last desperate refugees from the Nazi regime were seeking asylum on its shores. The well-organised 'illegal' immigration which ensued had some success (by 1947, 113,000 'illegal' immigrants had entered the country) but not enough for all to be saved and to avoid tragedy in the case of many.

The ending of the mandate in 1947, the Declaration of the Independence of the State of Israel on 14 May 1948 has not seen the end of violence. It has, however, given a home of their own to the scattered family, not only a refuge from the blows of the world but also *terra firma* on which to build a lasting future. The next family album must open in Israel . . .

GHETTO AND SHTETL

'Schwer zu sein ein Yid' ('It's hard to be a Jew') runs the old Yiddish tag. It has in fact a double meaning. It implies not only that the injunctions contained in the Jewish religion are difficult to fulfil, but also that the hardships the external world inflicts on the Jewish people are not conducive to an easy existence.

In the latter meaning, it hails from Eastern Europe. Life for the Jews there in modern times has always been hard. Today, we are particularly aware of the suffering the ideological doctrines of the Soviet Union place upon them. The same ideology of the Russian Revolution which brought them equality with all other national groups in the state, is today responsible for restrictions which prevent them practising their religion or their professions freely, which prevent them emigrating to Israel and cause them to be victimised if they apply for visas so to do.

In pre-revolutionary days, their sufferings were of a more basic physical and economic nature. Confined within the bounds of the Pale of Settlement, living in the small villages (the shtetls) in overcrowded conditions where there was never enough work, enough food, enough room for the ever-increasing population to live, it was indeed hard to be a Jew. Moreover, there was hardly an event in the external political world for which the Jews were not held responsible, blamed and used as scapegoats. To their intense poverty was added the fear of attack from without, the pogroms which could, for no apparent reason, descend upon them and, in a blind outburst of cruelty and violence, destroy their homes, friends, families, selves, and desecrate their synagogues, the scrolls of their Law.

They could not attack in a more vulnerable area. To the East European Jew, the great sustaining force in life was his religion. Throughout his suffering and pain, he was supported by the strength of his faith and his profound belief in God and His Law.

It was this combination of deep religious commitment and economic penury and physical fear that made Eastern Europe the breeding ground for every type of doctrine of religious and politico-revolutionary hope. From the material present, the East European Jew constantly sought escape in hope of a glorious future.

It is not surprising, therefore, that most of the major ideological movements that influenced world Jewry originated or attracted greatest support, in Eastern Europe. Here many false Messiahs won most of their followers. Here, as we have said, the doctrine of practical Zionism was born. Between the false Messiahs and Zionism, came a new message which spread through Eastern European Jewry like a flame, which left a permanent imprint on attitudes and which still burns brightly in a few isolated but strong communities to this day, in London, New York, Jerusalem.

The founder of the new doctrine of Hasidism (Pietism), Israel ben Eliezer, later known as the Baal Shem Tov (Master of the Good Name) was born in Eastern Europe in around 1700. An itinerant preacher who journeyed from village to village, he brought a message of joyous hope to the physically down-trodden Jews. The humble and pure of heart, he taught, however poor, however ignorant, however lowly, had as great or even a greater chance of happiness in the hereafter as the learned scholar, proud in his knowledge. For intellect was not in the last resort the prime factor. It was with the heart that God must be praised, and praised in joy, with dancing, singing, laughing, rejoicing. And why should one not rejoice? Was not the world beautiful? Was not everything beautiful as God had created all?

It is this doctrine which shines in the faces of the Jews in the pictures in this chapter. For them, it was not religiously hard to be a Jew. It was a permanent source of comfort and even of ecstasy.

19

A wayside encounter in a Galician country-lane, about 1895

Peasants in the village of Uschitza, near Zhitomir, 1928

At rest on the verandah, Ukraine, 1930

During the Festival of Tabernacles, a part of the roof is open to the sky and the opening covered with leaves and fruits.
Hungary, 1910

Market-day in
Strij, Galicia,
1905

Left: Musical accompaniment to the rabbi's wedding, Galicia, 1930
Below: Street scene in Sadowa-Wisznia, Galicia, 1900

Two Jews from Galicia. The man on the left wears a 'streimel', the flat hat trimmed with fur worn by the observant, about 1930

Overleaf, left: The fortress-style synagogue of Zolkiew, Galicia
Overleaf, right: In the synagogue, wearing phylacteries and prayer-shawl

Kasimiercz, the Jewish suburb of Cracow, 1890. Foreground right, the synagogue

33   Jews in Cracow, wearing the 'streimel' and caftan of the observant, about 1925

Open-air debate, about 1930

Waiting for the odd job at a street corner in a town in Eastern Poland, about 1928.
The street-sign is in Polish in Latin script; the writing on the wall is
in Russian in Cyrillic script; and the posters are in Hebrew

Market-day in Kasimiercz, 1925

Above: The Ringplatz at Oswiecim in Western Poland, 1905, later
to acquire terrible repute under its German name, Auschwitz

37

Right: Selling shoe polish and matches in the streets of Lodz, 1900

Above: Market-day in Rawa
Ruska, Galicia, 1910
Right: Street-trader, Lodz, 1900

38

Blacksmith at work, 1930

Galician villager, 1930

Tinker, 1930

41

Bootmaker and cobbler, 1930

Top: Between prayers in the synagogue, 1925
Facing: Interior of the synagogue, Przemysl, Galicia, 1900

Studying the Talmud, Vilna, Lithuania, 1910

Right: Studying the Talmud, Piaseczna, Poland, about 1930
Below: Hebrew School, Tyrnava, Slovakia, about 1930

A scroll of the Law is taken to the bedside of the sick, Munkács, Carpatho-Ukraine, about 1930

Grave-stone placed against the side of a house. The photograph above does not belong to the grave. From the Vilna-Grodno region

Outside the synagogue of Przemysl, 1905

50

Facing, top: Rzeszow, 1908
Facing, bottom: Conversation on a park bench, St Joachimsthal, Transsylvania, 1925
Above: A Jewish family in Galicia celebrates Passover, 1915, with two members of the Austrian Imperial Army

The rabbi's daugther, Galicia, 1928

Above: Street scene, Kolomea, 1914
Facing: Talmud student reads out a decree of the Austrian Imperial Army during maneuvres in Galicia, 1912

Below: Mural in the wooden synagogue of Peczenizyn, eastern Poland

56

The seventeenth-century wooden synagogue of Gwozdziecz, eastern Poland. Wooden synagogues were widespread in the area between Lodz in the west and the Ukraine (Kiev, Minsk)

ובנוחה יאמר שובה יֵ רבבות אפי ישרא קומה יֵ למנוחתיך אתה וארון עוזך כהניך ילבשו צדק וחסידיך דנך ירננו בעבור דוד עבדיך אל תשב פני משיחך בי לקח טוב נתתי לכם תורתי ואל תעזובו

...אמן בעלם הזה ובעולם הבא... ...כל שבעה...

59 *Facing:* Roof construction of the wooden synagogue, Wolpa, eastern Poland, built in the first half of the seventeenth century
Above: Painted ceiling of the synagogue, Gwozdziecz, according to an inscription of 1652, painted by Israel son of Mordecai

In front of the synagogue, Vladimir Volynsk, eastern Poland, 1914

61

Street scene, Lublin, Poland, 1914

Facing: Street-sweeper, Vladimir Volynsk, 1914
Above: At the village well, Vladimir Volynsk, 1914
63   *Right:* Galician peasant

Above: Jewish poverty in Eastern Europe. Note the dilapidated state of the roofs
Facing: In the Jewish quarter of Zborow, 1915

Above: Family group, Jedrzejow, 1915
Facing: On the main square, Sokolov, eastern Poland, 1915

Porters,
Vladimir Volynsk, 1914

At the turn of the nineteenth and twentieth centuries there were Yiddish theatrical troupes in Moscow, Kiev, Odessa, Vilna, Kishinev and other Jewish centres

Below: The Spirakowski-Samuel Adler Yiddish troupe in Kiev, 1908
Facing top: Mobile advertisement for the Yiddish Theatre in Warsaw
Facing bottom: Scene from a production of the Habimah Theatre in Moscow, founded in 1917. Here the language used was Hebrew, not Yiddish as elsewhere. Habimah moved to Palestine in 1931 and is now the National Theatre of Israel

After the pogrom in Kischinev, Bessarabia, during Easter, 1903
At least forty-nine Jews were killed and five hundred injured

גנוזת ספרי התורה הנקרעים
בעת הפרעות בקעשנוב י"ג מנחם אב תר סג

73   Solemn burial of the desecrated Scrolls of the Law

Jews in flight from Russia find shelter in Austrian
Lemberg, June 1882

A villager salvages a few possessions from the wreckage of his home, destroyed on the Eastern Front in the First World War 76

Galician Jews in flight from Tsarist troops, 1914–15

After the battle villagers trek back to their homes, 1914–15

In the shtetls of Eastern Europe, the Jew was first and foremost a Jew. The idea that he was a citizen of Russia only gained any meaning at all at times of crisis, when he was called, for example, to fight for his country against the armies of Napoleon. He spoke a different language from the other peoples of Russia. The books or the music he created were specifically Jewish works dealing with Jewish subjects.

This was definitely not the case with the emancipated Jews of Western Europe. As their affluence, prominence and assimilation increased, so they became more and more consciously citizens of that country. Similarly, they became less and less conscious of their Jewishness, to the extent often of converting to the dominant religion. Franz Kafka's novels are the novels of a Czech, only Jewish to the extent that the Jewish experience of alienation is universal. Offenbach's music is purely Parisian. Arthur Schnitzler's plays are the plays of a Viennese. When a Jew entered politics, he did so as a member of an existing political party and not in his role as a Jew. Benjamin Disraeli was leader of the British Conservative Party. The Jew lurking behind the Prime Minister was a secondary feature.

It is therefore impossible to speak of an overall Jewish culture in relation to Western Europe, as it is in the case of the East. There were only Jewish citizens of the various states. However, there were indubitably certain trends which were common to all. Of prime importance amongst these, was the tremendous upsurge in all branches of the arts and commerce which produced such names as Franz Werfel and Giacomo Meyerbeer; Sigmund Freud and Sarah Bernhardt; Gustav Mahler and Max Reinhardt. In all the major European communities, Jews seemed to be moving into the front ranks of creativity and contributing actively to the cultural development of their adopted country, if not of the world.

Another common trend was the movement towards urbanisation, which brought Jews in ever-growing numbers out of the small towns and villages of the countryside to seek their fortunes amidst the expanding opportunities offered by the capital cities. The Jewish populations of the glamorous, dignified, romantic Western capitals – Vienna, Prague, Paris, Amsterdam, Berlin – grew, as the nineteenth century advanced. From the relatively minimal levels of earlier times, quite sizable communities appeared.

In this milieu, the assimilated, emancipated Jews, the Jews who succeeded, grew rich, made money and a reputation for themselves, could live as well or better than the native Viennese, Parisian, Czech or German. They maintained substantial town houses furnished in the current massive, over-ornate taste with a thousand costly objects, moved with their families to the fashionable resorts over the holiday periods, ran carriages and horses, and cultivated a lively interest in music and the arts. To see them in their photographs, sipping tea at café tables, lounging elegantly on garden benches, dressed expensively in the fashions of the day, there is nothing to indicate that they are members of the Jewish family.

The international aspects of this phenomenon, as well as the peak to which affluence could raise the Western European Jew, was personified in the Rothschild family. With branches of the immensely powerful firm in most European capitals, the members of the family carried sumptuous living to new heights. The magnificent houses in Vienna or Paris, their country houses which are almost palaces in the English countryside, can still be seen today. Here, the various members of the close-knit family watched over the family fortunes, brought home their exquisite brides (who were themselves very frequently also Rothschilds), and indulged every conceivable whim, ranging from private zoos to private railways, from collecting every known species of the flea to driving carriages drawn by teams of zebras.

But while Jewish society in these capitals sparkled with artistic brilliance and gracious living, there was in the background a permanent reminder of what Jewish identity implied. It could take the form of the chain across the road which marked the entrance to the old ghetto at Eisenstadt or the actual ghetto itself in Prague. It might exist in the community of poor Jews who haunted certain quarters of these affluent cities: the London East End or the Jewish district in Vienna's inner city; the street market in Prague's Jewry or a slum in Amsterdam. The contrast they formed with the gracious boulevards and leafy avenues was too great to be ignored. Equally evocative were the groups of traditional religious Jews who still existed in parts of these cities, wearing the traditional garb.

They were the other side of the coin. They were objects of embarrassment, shame or guilt to their emancipated, westernised brethren. But they could not be ignored. The universal tendency towards philanthropy which characterised many of the leading Jewish citizens of the time may have been a means of expiating this guilt. It took a variety of forms. Frequently, once the doctrine of Zionism had gained ground, it was towards the promised land of Palestine that their attention was directed. Baron Edmond de Rothschild founded a number of colonies in the Holy Land, and continued to give financial assistance to many others. The English Jew, Sir Moses Montefiore, was a pioneer in his support of practical Zionism. But he was also continually aware of the hardships suffered by his Jewish brethren overseas. He intervened in the Damascus affair in 1841, and in various other episodes involving Jews in Eastern Europe, Turkey, Morocco and Rumania. Baron Maurice de Hirsch was another champion of East European Jewry, giving practical financial support to settlements in North and South America, particularly Argentina and Brazil.

Their efforts no doubt brought considerable improvements to their poorer co-religionists. No doubt philanthropy also made it easier for them to bear their own wealth. They could not ward off the disaster that was in the following century to strike the emancipated, assimilated, Western European Jew. Their wealth and their achievements turned to ashes in Hitler's holocaust.

The Ringstrasse in Vienna, about 1870

View of the Kärntnerstrasse.
Left, the Court Opera, in the background St Stephen's Cathedral, right the Palais Todesco

Eduard Freiherr von Todesco (1814–87) (sitting). The Todesco family, of Sephardi origin, were bankers, industrialists and railway entrepreneurs. Eduard's father, Hermann, the founder of the family's fortune, was raised to the Austrian nobility for his services to the state

Eduard's brother, Moritz Ritter von Todesco (1816–73)

Friedrich Freiherr von Schey-Koromla (1815–81).
Banker, railway entrepreneur and president of the
Vienna Chamber of Commerce. A great patron of
the arts, especially music and the theatre

Jonas Freiherr von Königswarter (1807–71), one of the most important bankers and
industrialists of his time. He was president of the Jewish community

Caryatids at the entrance to the Palais Epstein on the Burgring. It is now
the seat of the Vienna School administration

Vienna old and new, about 1880. Behind the remains of the Schottentor (front left) the Palais Ephrussi and the Votive Church.
The Ephrussi originated in Greece and Russia and were prominent in the banking world

Interior of the Villa Wertheimstein in Döbling, near Vienna. The Wertheimstein family was directly descended from Samson Wertheimer (1658–1724), financial adviser to the Habsburg Emperors Leopold I, Joseph I and Charles VI, and patron of Jewish scholarship

Emma von Ephrussi

Adolph von Sonnenthal (1834–1909). Born in Budapest he became one of the best known actors and mimes of the Vienna Burgtheater

Facing, top: Johann Strauss the Younger playing cards in the garden of his country home. His great-grandfather was Jewish; the entry in the baptismal register of St Stephen's was removed by the Nazis. To the left of the composer, his third wife Adèle
Facing, below: Johann Strauss and Adèle in an open carriage

Facing: Interior of the Vienna Opera

Above: Gustav Mahler (1860–1911) on his way to the opera. The son of a Jewish innkeeper in Moravia, he became director of
the Vienna Court Opera in 1897 (following his conversion to Catholicism). He resigned in 1907. Today Mahler is best known
for his ten symphonies but in his lifetime was more highly regarded as a conductor

Above: Felix Salten (1867–1945), Viennese journalist and author of the children's classic *Bambi*
Facing: Arthur Schnitzler (1862–1931) with his wife Olga and children Heinrich and Lily, photographed in 1910. Schnitzler, trained as a doctor, is best known for his plays, short stories and novels depicting *fin de siècle* Vienna

Top left: Karl Kraus (1874–1936), greatest satirist in modern German literature. For more than a quarter of a century his journal, *Die Fackel*, most of it written by Kraus himself, waged a sustained polemic against the follies, crimes and abuses of the contemporary world

Top right: Peter Altenberg (1859–1919), master of the short impressionistic prose sketch, the Vienna coffee-house litterateur *par excellence*

Left: Arnold Schönberg (1874–1951) whose twelve-tone technique revolutionised twentieth-century music

Top: Vienna, café in the Ringstrasse, 1915
Right: Egon Friedell (1878–1938), here shown on stage. But he was equally well known as cabaret artist, composer of epigrams and writer of cultural history. He committed suicide after the Anschluss with Germany in 1938

Above: Joseph Roth (1894–1939). The collapse of the Habsburg
Monarchy was the central experience of his life, and a theme to
which he repeatedly returned in his novels. He died in exile in
Paris
Right: The young Ferenc Molnár (1878–1952). The son of a
Budapest doctor, he won world fame as author of innumerable
light comedies

Corpus Christi Day procession in St Stephen's Square, Vienna.
Opposite the cathedral stood the department store of Jacob Rothberger.
The windows were hired out (as here) for special occasions

The old Jewish cemetery in the Seegasse, Vienna, about 1898

Sigmund Freud (1856–1939)

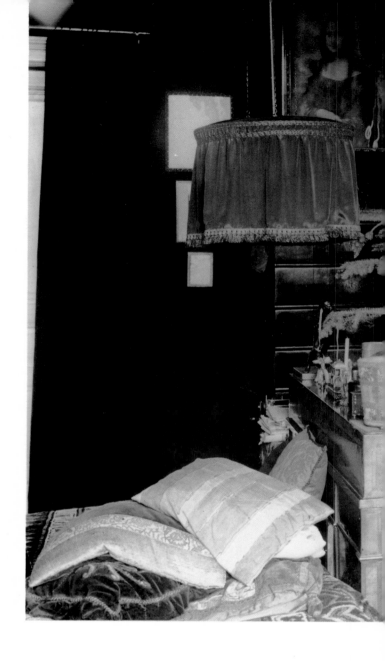

Top: Freud's study and consulting room, Berggasse 19
Right: Arthur Schnitzler's (see page 97) writing desk

Max Reinhardt (1873–1943), whose theatrical productions at Berlin and the Salzburg Festival made drama history. His name will also always be associated with the 'Theater in der Josefstadt'. The picture above shows Richard Strauss (third from left) in conversation with Reinhardt at the opening

Facing, top: Max Reinhardt's production of Goldoni's *A Servant of Two Masters* at the Salzburg Festival, 1926
Facing, below: During a rehearsal at the Salzburg Festival, 1925. Left, the poet of *Jedermann*, Hugo von Hofmannsthal (1875–1929) who together with Richard Strauss and Max Reinhardt (middle) founded the Salzburg Festival after the First World War

In the Jewish quarter of the inner town, Vienna, 1915

Old ghetto houses in Leopoldstadt, Vienna, about 1900

Rabbi and wife, Vienna, 1865

Street-traders in the Vienna flea-market, 1910

Galician Jews in Vienna, 1915, seeking safety from the battlefields of the Eastern front

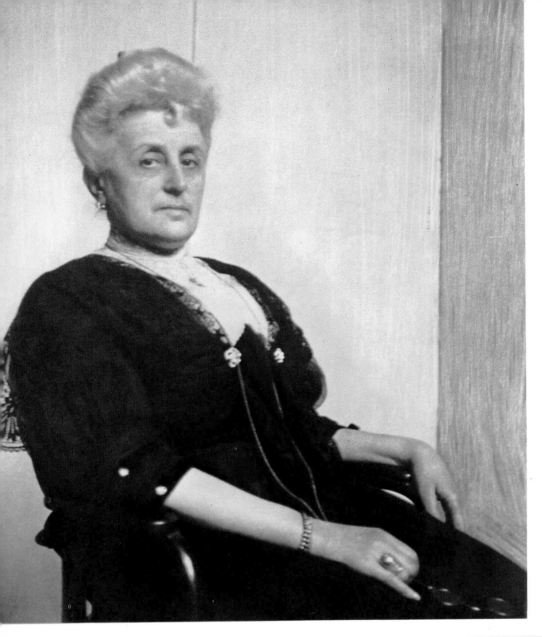

From the album of the Niernstein family
Top: Grandma
Right: Ancestral portraits over father's desk

Top: The children in the garden:
sailor suits and soldiers' shakos for the boys;
dirndl dresses for the girls
Right: On the way to school

Right: In the mountains
Below: Family excursion

Left: In search of the simple life
Below: Reichenau an der Rax, favourite summer
resort for the Viennese upper middle class

Top: Jewish cemetery in Eisenstadt, before
1915
Right: Entrance to the old ghetto in Eisenstadt. Note the Hebrew lettering over the gate

A chain, hung over the street, separated the Eisenstadt ghetto from
the rest of the town until 1938

PRAGUE

Street market in the Jewish quarter,
about 1900

Left: Janitor of the old Pinkas Synagogue
in Prague
Below: The old cemetery
Facing: Inner view of the Pinkas Synagogue
to the south-east

Top: At the junction of Graben and the
Wenzelsplatz – favourite meeting place of the
Germans in Prague, about 1910
Left: Max Brod (1884–1968). Man of letters and
friend of Kafka whose unpublished manuscripts
he preserved for posterity, Brod was an early
supporter of Zionism and went to Palestine
in 1939

Franz Kafka (1883–1924), whose novels reveal the existential predicament of modern man

Franz Werfel (1890–1945). Born in Prague, and bound by friendship to Kafka and Brod, Werfel became an exponent of expressionism in German lyric poetry. He was married to Mahler's widow

In the Prague ghetto

Above: Mobile coffee-stall, 1905
Overleaf: The Meiselgasse in Prague with the thirteenth-century Old-New Synagogue and the sixteenth-century Jewish Town Hall. Note the lower clock dial with Hebrew numerals. The hands move anti-clockwise

Rue de Rivoli, built 1806–35.
Right, the Tuileries and the Louvre

Right: The Péreire family, 1880. Jacob Émile Péreire, descended from a Portuguese Sephardi family, was president of the Crédit Mobilier, at one time a rival to the Rothschilds. Jacob's grandfather, Rodrigues, was a pioneer in the education of deaf-mutes
Below: Eugène Péreire

Left: The classical front of the Nissim de Camondo museum in Paris, formerly the town mansion of Count Moses de Camondo (1860–1935), son of Isaac. The mansion with its superb collection of French art of the eighteenth and nineteenth centuries, was bequeathed to the Louvre in memory of Nissim de Camondo, killed in an air battle in the First World War
Facing: The writing room

Above: Isaac de Camondo, Turkish-Jewish financier and philanthropist
Right: Nissim de Camondo (1892–1917)

Facing: Jacques Offenbach (1819–80). Born in Cologne, he lived in Paris from the age of sixteen. His operettas *(La Belle Hélène, Orpheus in the Underworld, Tales of Hoffmann)* brought him world fame and created the legend of gay Paris
Above: Sarah Bernhardt (1845–1923). One of the first international stars of the theatre

Top: The Paris Opera House. A stereoscope picture of 1903

Bottom right: Giacomo Meyerbeer (1791–1864). Born in Berlin as Jacob Liebmann Beer, he went to Italy in 1816 and settled in Paris in 1826. He was the chief representative of French grand opera in the mid-nineteenth century

Bottom left: Jacques Halévy (1799–1862) won world fame with his grand opera *La Juive* (1835)

Sarah Bernhardt in her boudoir. Every item – curtains, cushions, rugs, leopard skins – is redolent of 'la belle époque'

Thadée Natanson, patron
of the arts, publisher of the
Revue Blanche (1891–1903),
Spokesman of the symbolist
poets and the group of
painters known as the Nabis
(Bonnard, Vuillard, etc.)

Natanson and Misia Sert

Afternoon coffee with
Florent Fels (centre), one of the
pioneers of the modern movement
in art. Standing, Marc Chagall and,
extreme right, Bella, Chagall's
model and later his wife

Marc Chagall in his Paris studio. Chagall, born in White Russia in 1889, first moved to Paris in 1910. A rebel against orthodox realism, his work combines whimsicality with influences drawn from Hasidism and Russian popular art

Stage producer Léon Bakst (right), Chagall's teacher in Paris, with Stravinsky (sitting) and Larinov, 1898

Above: Gertrude Stein's work room. Note the walls hung with the work of some of the most important contemporary painters
Right: Gertrude Stein (1874–1946). Born in America of a German-Jewish family she lived in Paris from 1902. Important both as writer and mentor to 'the lost generation' of American writers living in voluntary exile in France after 1918, such as Hemingway

143   Daniel-Henry Kahnweiler, born in 1844 in Mannheim. For a time he held an exclusive contract to handle Picasso's work

Facing: La Rûche (the Beehive), originally a pavilion at the World Exhibition in Paris, later transformed into a home for artists to work and live in
Above: In the Café du Dome, Montparnasse. In the centre, Jules Pascin (1885–1930), born in Bulgaria

Chaim Soutine (1893–1942), born in Lithuania, lived in Paris from 1913

Moise Kisling (1891–1953), born in Cracow, lived in Paris from 1910

Adolphe Basler (right) the critic, in the Café du Dome; next to him Amedeo Modigliani (1884–1920) from a Sephardi
family of Leghorn

Facing: Umbrella-salesman in the streets of Paris

Above: Captain Dreyfus (right) promoted to Major after his rehabilitation in 1906. Dreyfus (1859–1935), a captain on the French general staff, was falsely condemned in 1894 on charges of high treason and exiled to Devil's Island

Left: André Citroën (right) in conversation with an American trade union leader, 1918

THE ROTHSCHILDS

Left: Mentmore in Buckinghamshire near London was acquired by Mayer Amschel Rothschild, a brother of Nathaniel (see page 153), in 1851. Mayer Amschel's only child, his daughter Hannah, married Lord Rosebery, British Prime Minister 1894–5

Below: Lunch party given by Baron Edward Rothschild (1868–1949) at the Derby at Epsom, 1909

Page 150: Nathaniel Rothschild (1812–70) of the second generation of the English branch of the family, photographed in 1865
Page 151: Family house of the Rothschilds in the Judengasse in Frankfurt on Main. Mayer Amschel Rothschild (1744–1812) founded the banking house. His four sons established independent branches in London, Paris, Vienna and Naples
Below: Ascot Races, 1913. Left in picture, Mrs Leopold de Rothschild (1862–1937)

Top: Main façade of the town house built by Baron Albert Rothschild (1844–1911) on the Prinz-Eugen-Strasse in Vienna
Bottom left: Albert Freiherr von Rothschild, third head of the Vienna branch
Bottom right: Charlotte Beatrix Baroness de Rothschild (1864–1934)
Facing: Countess Kitty Schönborn-Buchheim (1885–1946) later the wife of Eugene Freiherr von Rothschild, of the Austrian branch of the family. After his abdication in 1936, Edward VIII stayed at their castle at Enzesfeld near Vienna

154

Top: Ferrières-en-Brie near Paris, one of the prize possessions of the French Rothschilds. At one time it contained a private zoo and miniature railway
Right: Alfred Charles de Rothschild (1842–1918) of the English branch of the family. Dandy, aesthete and eccentric, he maintained his own symphony orchestra and private circus. He served for twenty-one years on the council of the Bank of England

156

Mayer Alphonse de Rothschild (1827–1905), second head of the
Paris branch, in 1878

Leonora de Rothschild (1837–1911). She married
her cousin Mayer Alphonse

Left: Waddesden Manor, the luxurious country seat built by Ferdinand James (1839–98), one of the Vienna Rothschilds. Ferdinand became an English citizen and Member of Parliament for Aylesbury. Waddesden is a repository of many very precious art treasures, some of the most notable coming from French Renaissance châteaux

Below: Lionel Walter Rothschild (1868–1937), the second baron, Zionist and recipient of the Balfour Declaration in 1917. He was also a distinguished naturalist and owned a private zoo

Facing, top: The famous zebra four-in-hand of Lionel Walter Rothschild, the second baron
Facing, below: Sir Anthony Rothschild (1810–76) was an English baronet as well as an Austrian baron
Facing, below right: James ('Jimmy') Armand de Rothschild (1878–1956), a member of the French branch of the family. He became an English citizen and Liberal Member of Parliament. Art connoisseur and devotee of the track

Above: The Houses of Parliament with Big Ben, 1892
Right: David Lindo Alexander, President of the Board of Deputies, the representative body of Anglo-Jewry, whose origins go back to the eighteenth century. Alexander was one of the signataries of a letter to *The Times* in May 1917 opposing the steps being taken towards the eventual issue of the Balfour Declaration

LONDON

Sir George Jessel (1824–83), crowned his legal career by his appointment as Solicitor General in 1871 in Gladstone's cabinet, the first Jew to become a Minister of the Crown

Rufus Daniel Isaacs (1860–1935) first Marquess of Reading. Attorney-General, 1910, Lord Chief Justice, 1913, Viceroy of India, 1920, Foreign Secretary, 1931. Associated with several Zionist projects including Palestine Electric Corporation

Sir David Salomons (1797–1873) one of the first English Jews to receive a title. Founder of the Westminster Bank, Member of Parliament and Lord Mayor of London. Photographed in 1865

Dr Nathan Marcus Adler (1803–90),
Chief Rabbi 1844–89

Interior of the Hambro Synagogue, which was established in London in 1707 and stood until 1936. The Hambro family came to England from Norway

Benjamin Disraeli, Earl of Beaconsfield (1804–81). Born of a Sephardi family, baptised 1817. One of the greatest Conservative statesmen of the nineteenth century. As a not inconsiderable novelist he handled both romantic and realistic themes

Queen Victoria (1819–1901)
and the Prince Consort, Albert of Saxe-Coburg-Gotha. Photo by Roger Fenton, 1854

Demonstration in London's East
End protesting against anti-Jewish
persecution in Poland, 1919

E APPEAL
REAT BRITAIN
OP THE BUTCHERY
EWS IN POLAND
WE PROTEST AGAINST
THE CONTINUED SLAUGHTER
OF INNOCENT JEWISH
WOMEN AND CHILDREN
IN POLAND.

168

Facing: Rufus Daniel Isaacs
Above: London Stock Exchange, 1892

Sir Frederick John Goldsmid (1818–1908), distinguished orientalist, became a general in the service of the Khedive of Egypt

Colonel Albert Edward W. Goldsmid

Sommerhill, near Tonbridge, the country seat of Colonel H. D'Avigdor Goldsmid, 1926

Hughenden in Buckinghamshire, Disraeli's country seat

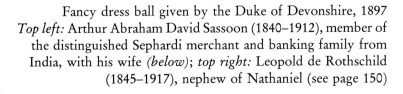

Fancy dress ball given by the Duke of Devonshire, 1897
Top left: Arthur Abraham David Sassoon (1840–1912), member of
the distinguished Sephardi merchant and banking family from
India, with his wife *(below); top right:* Leopold de Rothschild
(1845–1917), nephew of Nathaniel (see page 150)

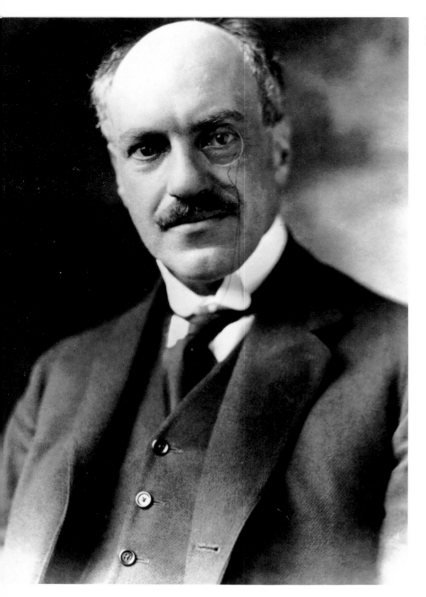

Edwin Samuel Montagu (1879–1924), English politician and
Secretary of State for India (1917–22)

Sir Jack Benn Brunel Cohen (1886–1965), Treasurer of the
British Legion

Left: Sir Ernest Cassel (1852–1921). English banker of German origin, close friend of Edward VII. Shown here in the regalia of the Order of St Michael and St George

Below: Party at Viscount Samuel's (1870–1963). The Liberal statesman was High Commissioner for Palestine from 1920 to 1925. Centre, standing, Samuel; extreme right, James de Rothschild (see page 158)

Street scene in London's East End

Facing, top: Banquet of the Jewish Historical Society in 1906, to celebrate the 250th anniversary of the re-admission of the Jews to England under Cromwell
Facing, below, left: Sir Marcus Samuel (1853–1927), later Viscount Bearsted, founder of the Shell Oil Company
Facing, below, right: Lady Samuel

Above: Country seat of Sir Moses Montefiore in Ramsgate, Kent
Facing: Sir Moses Montefiore (1784–1885) was born in Leghorn of a Sephardi family. He won a world-wide reputation in the nineteenth century as defender of threatened Jewry – whether in Russia, Turkey, Morocco or Rumania. He also founded the Jewish colony, Yemin Moshe, in Jerusalem

THE PHILANTHROPISTS

Montefiore settlement in Jerusalem, about 1875

Sir Moses travelling carriage in the procession on his 100ʳᵈ birthday.

Left: Baron Edmond de Rothschild
(1845–1934) on a visit to Palestine, where he
founded four colonies and supported a
number of others. Before 1914
Below: Rosh Pinah, founded by colonists
from Russia, 1912

182

183

Above: Co-operative shop in Moisesville in
Santa Fé Province, Argentina, 1924
Left: Baron Maurice de Hirsch (1831–96),
German financier and philanthropist. His
benefactions did much to assist the re-settlement
of Jews from Eastern Europe in North and
South America, especially Argentina and Brazil

Above: Street in Moisesville, 1904
Facing, top: Group picture from Argentina, about 1910. In the foreground two Jewish gauchos
Facing, below: Jewish gauchos pose with Argentine colleagues. Mauricio, Buenos Aires Province, Argentina

184

185

The Muiderstraat
in the old Jewish quarter

186

Sabbath peace

Top: Second-hand clothing store
Left: In the slums of the Jewish quarter of
Amsterdam

Top: Sunday morning in
the Jewish district
Right: Burning the last
remnants of leaven before
189   the Festival of Passover

Beggars at the New Synagogue in the Jonas Daniel Meijersplein

In the Jewish quarter.
Anne Frank was concealed in a building such as this

Above: The Amsterdam jeweller Izak Lamon, former ward of the Jewish Orphanage, with his sons
Below: The Diamond Bourse in Weesperplein

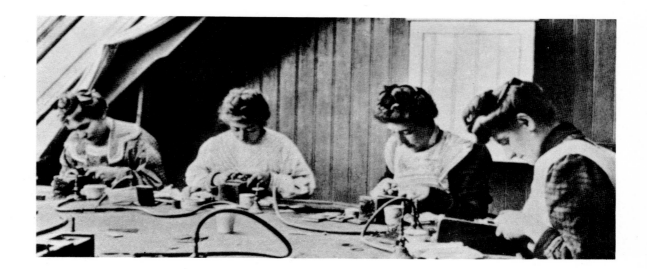

Above: The Dutch queen visits the Portuguese Synagogue, 1904
Left: David de Raphael Montezinos, a benefactor of the Portuguese Synagogue, and J. S. da Silva Rosa, prominent member of the Amsterdam Jewish community

From the golden age of Hollywood. Left to right, N. Lasky, Adolph Zukor, Samuel Goldwyn, Cecil B. de Mille and Boris Kaufmann, brother of the Soviet *avant-garde* artiste Dsiga Vertov (see also pages 202–3)

FROM THE
WORLD OF FILM

Above: Adolph Zukor, film magnate
Facing: Entrance to the Paramount Cinema Palace, New York, at the end of the 1920s

Above: Groucho Marx
Facing, top: Typical scene from a Marx Brothers film. *Left*, Chico, *centre*, Groucho, *right*, Harpo
Facing, below: Erich von Stroheim (1885–1957). Born in Vienna, he went to the United States in 1907. Film
director, but best known for his portrayals of Prussian officer types

Josef von Sternberg, one of the directors of the great age of the
German film company, Ufa. Discovered Marlene Dietrich

Erich Pommer
Joe May

Two Ufa star producers:
Erich Pommer and Joe May

Ernst Lubitsch (1892–1947), director of classic film comedies in Germany and, later, Hollywood. Left, Pola Negri

202

BERLIN

Facing: Fritzi Massary (1882–1969), Vienna-born operetta star who became the darling of Berlin
Below: Berlin at the turn of the century; Friedrichstrasse station

Above: Leopold Ullstein (1826–1899), from a daguerreotype of about 1860. Began as paper merchant, founded in 1877 a publishing house that developed into of Europe's largest
Facing: Hungarian-born Samuel Fischer (1859–1934). In 1886 he founded a publishing house that numbered amongst its authors Gerhart Hauptmann, Thomas Mann and Franz Kafka

Alfred Flechtheim (1878–1937),
art collector and dealer

Herwarth Walden (1878–1941), with his wife Nell,
in their Berlin home, 1920. Walden's journal *Der
Sturm* was the mouthpiece of the German
Expressionists

Einstein (1879–1955) with the violinist Bronislaw Hubermann (1882–1947)

The synagogue in the
Oranienburgstrasse, Berlin

In the Jewish quarter

Amateur theatricals

Max Liebermann (1847–1935) in his studio, 1900. He was the most important representative of Impressionism in Germany

Facing top left: Walther Rathenau (1867–1922), president of the German Electric Company (AEG) founded by his father Emil. During the First World War, director of the Raw Material Procurement Division in the German Ministry of War. As Foreign Minister of the Weimar Republic he was assassinated in 1922 by right-wing anti-semitic extremists

Facing top right: Wertheim department store, built in 1904 by Adolf Messel

Facing below: Tietz department store, on the Alexanderplatz, 1928

Two stars of stage and screen: the tenor Richard Tauber (1892–1948) and the soubrette Gitta Alpar

Ernst Lubitsch (see page 201) on stage with Ossi Oswalda. Lubitsch began his acting career with Reinhardt

Carl Sternheim (1878–1942), biting satirist of the philistinism of Wilhelmine Germany, here
shown at his marriage with Pamela Wedekind in 1930

Three conductors

Top left: Bruno Walter (1876–1962)
Top right: Otto Klemperer (1885–1972)
Right: Leo Blech (1871–1958)

216

Lion Feuchtwanger (1884–1958), best selling novelist of the 1920s and 1930s

Alfred Kerr (1867–1948), doyen of Berlin critics in the 1920s

From a family album

Main street in the ghetto of Frankfurt on Main in 1865. Background left, the synagogue. One side of the street was razed to allow for the expansion of the town

Carriage of Freiherr von Oppenheimer at Cologne race track

Mein Feld ist die Welt.

Albert Ballin (1857–1918), managing director of the mighty Hamburg–America shipping line. Here Ballin is accompanying the Kaiser to the launching of the *Bismarck*

Preceding pages: Emigrants waiting to leave, Hamburg, 1909

The speed with which the new immigrant integrates into American society is a marked feature of American life. Two or three generations and the penniless alien refugee, huddled on board the immigrant ship, dubiously scanning the unknown horizon, becomes the respectable, respected American citizen. Part of the explanation for the rapidity of the transformation lies, of course, in the character of America itself. It is a country in a sense made up entirely of immigrants, subject until recent times to continual waves of newcomers, each one a stranger, with strange customs, strange dress, strange language, strange religion. The Jew, in this medley, was no oddity — no odder in fact than any other new group. He was no aberration from an accepted norm because there was no accepted norm. Here, he was spared the conflict between his identity as a Jew and his identity as an American. He was fully able to take advantage of the vast opportunities for self-development and self-advancement the new world offered.

When the flood of Eastern European Jewish immigrants broke on the American shore, a community of German Jews was already established there. Some had been in residence since the end of the Napoleonic wars; by the 1880s, they numbered some 230,000 and many had reached positions of considerable eminence in American society and in political and commercial life. In New York, in particular, they already formed a circle of an entirely individual nature. They are the *Our Crowd* of Stephen Birmingham's book. They have sometimes been described as an 'aristocracy'. They did, in fact, create for themselves a world apart, secured by their enormous wealth and by intermarriage, a world of Fifth Avenue mansions, country houses and sumptuous entertaining on one hand; financial acumen and government service on another; and philanthropy on an unbelievable scale on a third. Their story is an admirable illustration of the Americanisation process at its best.

By the time of the American Civil War, there were already several Jewish banking houses in the United States established by these men who only a matter of years before had newly entered the country as German immigrants. The names of the firms they founded are today internationally renowned: August Belmont (who was the American agent for the Rothschilds); Speyer & Co. (founded in 1837); and J. and W. Seligman (1857). They were later joined by Kuhn, Loeb & Co. (1865); Lehman Brothers (1868); J. S. Bache & Co.; Ladenburg, Thalmann & Co.; and Goldman, Sachs & Co. It was on them that the American government depended for its finance during the American Civil War. Seligman's, run by several liberal-minded brothers, was particularly helpful and when peace had been declared, it continued to act as the government's official fiscal agent as well as to assist the Navy Department. Lehman's on the other hand, founded by the brothers Mayer and Emmanuel in Montgomery, Alabama, during the War, worked for the Confederacy and Jefferson Davis.

But Joseph Seligman had been born in Baiersdorf in Germany, and only appeared in New York for the first time in 1837. August Belmont was born August Schönberg in the Rhineland Palatinate in 1816.

Loeb was the son of a poor Worms wine merchant. Abraham Kuhn began life as a pedlar and later operated a factory manufacturing men's and boys' trousers. Henry Lehman was born in 1844 in Rimper, Bavaria, and reached Mobile in the USA as a pedlar with a wagon.

Their stories are matched by those of other members of the 'Crowd'. Mayer Guggenheim who emigrated from Switzerland at the age of nineteen, was a pedlar in a coal-mining and farming area of Pennsylvania. He tried out various other methods of making money before a fortunate investment in Colorado in 1890 started him on a career which led to his later fabulous wealth as a major world producer and smelter of copper, silver and other metals. Jacob Schiff (1847–1920) was born in Frankfurt but by 1885 had become head of Kuhn, Loeb and Company in New York. In 1897, he carried through the reorganisation of the Union Pacific Railroad Company and its merger with the Southern Pacific and other lines. His hatred for the Russian Tsarist government was so great that he floated a two-hundred-million dollar bond issue to help Japanese government during the Russo-Japanese war.

In fact, 'Our Crowd' were noted for their philanthropic activities. Otto Kahn for instance was a leading patron of the arts and music in the United States. As Chairman of the Metropolitan Opera House in New York he regularly supported its annual deficits, and also underwrote American tours by foreign companies — Diaghilev's Ballet Russe in 1918, the Moscow Arts Theatre under Stanislavsky in 1923, and Max Reinhardt's German productions in 1928. The Guggenheims did not lag behind: Solomon established his Foundation and Museum for Non-Objective Art in 1937, while another member of the tribe founded the John Simon Guggenheim Memorial Foundation to assist gifted artists, scientists and scholars with fellowships. Nathan Straus, one of the owners of the Macy Department Store empire, on the other hand, dealt in more practical philanthropy. An immigrant boy from Germany, raised in poverty in Talbottom, Georgia, he believed that charity was more beneficial if it were paid for. During periods of hardship, such as the hard winter of 1893–4, he opened depots for selling food and coal at five cents a package and lodging houses where for five cents, clean beds and warm breakfasts were provided. In 1914 he ran milk stations where for one cent, milk and sandwiches were served.

Other members of the crowd devoted themselves entirely to politics. Oscar S. Straus (1850–1926) held important government appointments under four Presidents of America, was ambassador to Turkey in 1887 and a member of Theodore Roosevelt's cabinet. Herbert Lehman was democratic Governor of New York for four terms from 1928. He supported Roosevelt's New Deal and was director of UNRRA during the Second World War. Later, he was a Senator for the State of New York.

They are a brilliant example of the American success story, these members of 'Our Crowd', proving to successive generations of new Jewish immigrants that a Jewish boy might not yet have become President, but he could get very near to it . . .

Page 227: The New World comes into view
Above: Registering Jewish passengers in the emigration halls of the Hamburg-America line, Hamburg-Weddel, about 1909

Emigrant ship leaves harbour. View of the forward deck of the SS *Blücher*. Hamburg-Weddel, about 1909

The embarkation

Arriving in New York

Facing, top: Ellis Island, about 1905
Facing, bottom: Immigration officials inspect the new arrivals
Below: Waiting in Ellis Island, about 1910

Immigrant family, Ellis Island, about 1920

239

Facing: Lower East Side: Hester Street at the turn of the century
Above: Scene in Hester Street

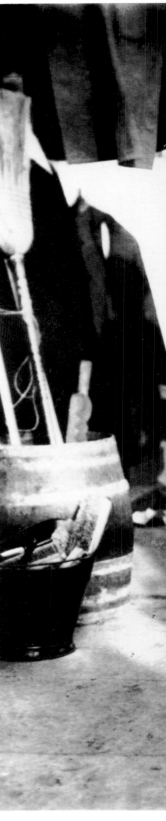

In the Jewish quarter of Brooklyn, 1899

Top left: On the way home after the Sabbath morning service, 1901
Top right: Galicia in Manhattan: Hat-seller, 1901
Bottom left: Jewish working-girls, 1901
Bottom right: Street traders
Facing: Street life between two high walls. Lower East Side, 1901

Facing: Cap-maker at work
Above: Sweated labour: Bohemian cigar-makers at work

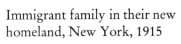
Immigrant family in their new homeland, New York, 1915

Hebrew elementary school in Hester Street, 1889

The Sabbath loaf – in a hovel in Ludlow Street (Lower East Side)

Above: Grand St Theatre, home of the Jewish stage in New York, about 1900
Facing, top: The cast of *Broken Hearts* with the producer Jacob Adler, about 1900
Facing, bottom left: Miss Bertha Kalisch, star of the Jewish theatre in America
Facing, bottom right: Abraham Goldfaden, director of the Jewish theatre in Jassy
(Bessarabia). From his troupe came the members of the Jewish theatre in New York

248

Left: The New Lyceum Theatre in 45th Street West, Manhattan, built by the producer Daniel Frohmann. New York, 1903

Bottom: Frohmann in his office, about 1905

Facing, top: Cinematograph Theatre in the Lower East Side, about 1912. The Hebrew poster on right advertises New Year services

Facing, bottom left: Theatrical producer David Belasco in his office, 1909. As a librettist Belasco was also very successful (Puccini's *Girl from the Golden West, Madam Butterfly*)

Facing, bottom right: David Belasco and Charles Frohmann, son of Daniel Frohmann, 1915

Billie Burke, Florence Ziegfeld's wife, on a poster
advertising the Ziegfeld Follies

Top left: Theatrical producer Florence Ziegfeld, whose Ziegfeld Follies were a
milestone in the history of show business
Top right: The Dolly Sisters, stars of the 1920s
Right: Irving Berlin, born in Russia in 1888. His 'White Christmas' became a
folk-song and 'God Bless America' a patriotic hymn

Top: The building of R. H.
Macy & Co. at the corner of Sixth
Avenue and 14th Street. Isidor
Straus, born in the Rhineland in
1845, entered the firm in 1888 and
bought it eight years later with his
younger brother Nathan. In 1902
Macy's was built on its present site
on Broadway (see page 256)
Right: Edward W. Bloomingdale,
the founder of Bloomingdale's, the
well-known store on Lexington
Avenue

Facing: Tobacco store on the Lower East
Side. An interesting example of the New
York 'melting pot'. The name of the
store is in English and Yiddish; the sign
in the shop windows has the Russian
two-headed eagle; and the traditional
'Cigar Store Indian' is replaced by a
Scotsman in kilt and tam o'shanter

Above: Broadway and Herald Square, Manhattan, 1912. Foreground left, Gimbel's; behind, Sak's, 34th Street, followed by Macy's

Facing: Bridal portrait of Alva Gimbel, daughter-in-law of Adam Gimbel, founder of the department store dynasty. The marriage took place in the ballroom of the Plaza Hotel, New York in 1912

Julius Ochs, born in Fürth, 1826, here shown as an officer of the northern states in the Civil War, 1861—5

Adolph S. Ochs, son of Julius, was twenty when he took over the Chattanooga *Times* in 1878. In 1896 he became publisher of the New York *Times* which he built into a journal of world affairs

Helena Rubinstein in a ball dress created by Worth. She was a young girl when she went from Poland to Australia and thence to America where she set new standards for the cosmetics industry

Otto M. Kahn, partner in the New York banking house of Kuhn, Loeb & Co., 1925

Metropolitan Opera House ('The Met'), beginning of the twentieth century

Right: Mayer Guggenheim, born in 1828 in German Switzerland, one of the pioneers of American industrialisation

Below: Simon Guggenheim (*left*), son of Mayer, who together with his wife (also in the picture) established the Guggenheim Foundation to further the Arts and Sciences

Fifth Avenue north of 65th Street, 1898

Top left: Bernard Baruch (1870–1965). The adviser to American presidents from Teddy Roosevelt (1901) to John F. Kennedy (1963)

Top right: Felix M. Warburg and wife. Through his marriage to Frieda Schiff he became a partner in his father-in-law's banking house, Kuhn, Loeb & Co.

Left: Ralph Pulitzer, 1899. Son of the Hungarian-born newspaper magnate Joseph Pulitzer, benefactor of the Pulitzer prizes for journalism

Right: Isaac Seligman of the New York banking family, whose origins go back to eight brothers who left Franconia for America about 1840

Below: The second generation: Mortimer Schiff and wife at the races. Mortimer, brother-in-law of Felix Warburg, was the son of Jacob Henry Schiff, who in his youth left Germany for New York to become director of Kuhn, Loeb & Co.

August Belmont Senior (Frenchified translation of Schönberg). He was twenty when he came to New York as an employee of the Rothschild's

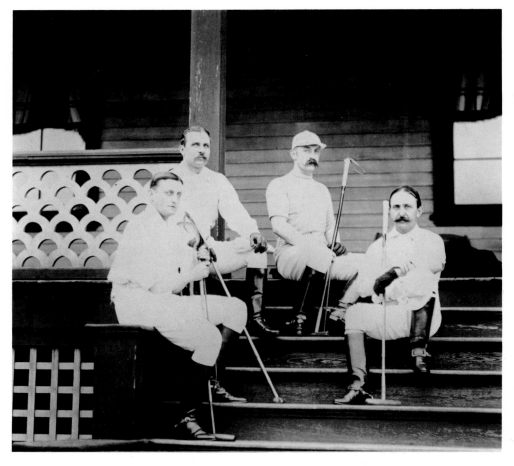

Above: Mrs August Belmont Senior in a coach
and four before her house in Newport, Rhode
Island
Right: August Belmont Junior (extreme right)
relaxing after a game of polo

Gould family's car park, 1906

New York *fin de siècle* banquet, 1900–1

The dispersion of 70 C. E. which scattered the Jewish family to the four corners of the world has been replaced by the beginnings of an ingathering. The Jews of the diaspora who, over the centuries, have acquired the characteristics of the nation amongst whom they have lived, are coming together once more in the land of Israel. They arrived as East European Hasidic Jews, German Jews, Jews from Bokhara, Yemenite rabbis, Kurdish Jews, Armenian Jews, Algerian Jews, Moroccan Jews . . . They often wore the national costume of their birth, spoke its language, and brought with them its national customs. They became Israeli citizens. It is the amalgam of all these diverse elements that will eventually form an Israeli national type.

Some things they had in common. There was the acknowledgment of their Jewishness, of their membership of the family, despite the great superficial difference that separated brother from brother. There was an innate, inbred yearning for the homeland inculcated by the religion and incarnated for many in the doctrine of Zionism. Finally, in the majority of cases, there was the driving force of persecution or fear of persecution.

The new state of Israel adopted a Western type of democracy—the only one of its kind in the Middle East. An ideological socialism inspired the early settlement of the land—the kibbutzim, the moshavim. Just as the ideal of the state is of a collective unity in which every Jew has a share and where the land is collectively owned, so the agricultural settlements are run on a collective basis. Whatever their later development, they began on a socialist programme of 'from each according to his ability; to each according to his need'. They created a closed moneyless society, where property did not exist, where even the children were raised in a communal children's house, and where the smaller family unit became dissolved in the larger. And all the time, their mental and physical effort was devoted to working the land, their land.

For the task of building up the country has been the primary concern of every settler since the earliest days. Agriculturally, there was the need to make the dry, neglected soil bring forth a living for the mouths that had to be fed, to make the desert bloom, to plant trees to anchor the sand to the rock, to bring water to an arid countryside. Commercially, plants had to be built to provide the elementary necessities of life, such as electricity, factories erected to produce manufactured goods, towns to be expanded or, like Tel Aviv, created. Over a period of less than a century since the first Zionist aliyah, Israel has changed from a backward, barren Middle Eastern land to a modern industrial state.

And still the building goes on. Still the attempts to integrate the diverse elements in the population continue. Still, unfortunately, the need remains to dissipate the country's energies in the over-riding necessity of defence. Still the Jews pray at the Wailing Wall, where their ancestors have prayed for centuries, for peace.

Theodor Herzl in his Vienna study with children Hans, Trude and Pauline

Second Zionist Congress in Basle, 1898

Left: In 1882 the *Thetis* brought the first Jewish colonists to Palestine

Below: A launch brings the colonists' possessions into Jaffa Harbour

Facing: In Jaffa Harbour. The man with the fez is a maritime official of the Jewish Agency

Left: A crowded emigration office in Warsaw, 1930

Below: The *Velos*, the first 'illegal' immigrant ship, 1934. It anchored off the coast in the open sea. The immigrants were brought secretly ashore in rowing boats. Picture taken by one of the immigrants

Facing: Before disembarkation in Haifa Harbour

Jerusalem: View of the Mount of Olives, 1865

P. Bergheim

Jerusalem: The Wailing Wall, 1873

Studying the Talmud in a Jerusalem synagogue, 1870

Persian Jew in Jerusalem, 1912

Traditionally garbed Polish Jews at the Jaffa Gate in Jerusalem, 1931

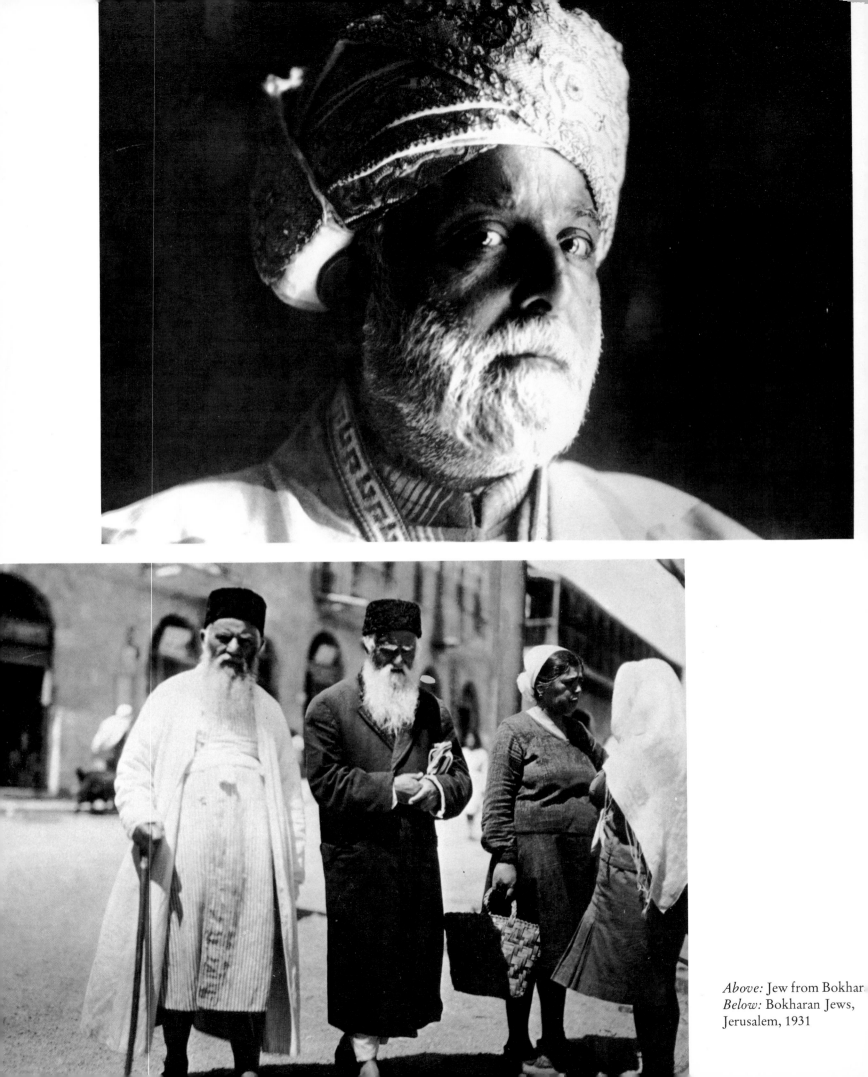

Above: Jew from Bokhar
Below: Bokharan Jews,
Jerusalem, 1931

Jewish quarter of the old City of Jerusalem, 1912. Bottom left, the Sephardi synagogue, top right, the Ashkenazi

Below: Kurdish Jew, Jerusalem, 1915
Facing: The Wailing Wall, Jerusalem, 1912

Yemenite craftsman, Jerusalem, 1914

Ashkenazi street traders, Jerusalem, 1931

Ashkenazi women at market, Jerusalem, 1931

Sephardi street trader, Jerusalem, 1931

Bokharan Jew, Jerusalem, 1931

Sephardi Jews, Jerusalem, 1931

Tel-Aviv was established on
the sand-dunes at Jaffa in 1909

The Tel-Aviv of 1920

Tel-Aviv about 1911. In the background, the twin towers of the city's most important structure – its water reservoirs

Interior of one of the huts of Kfar Hasidim, a collective settlement founded near Haifa in 1924 by Hasidim from Poland

Bringing in the harvest at Kfar Hasidim, 1926

The tented settlement of Beth Alpha in the Plain of Jezreel.
In the background, Mount Gilboa

Deganyah, the first kibbutz, founded in 1909

The dairy farm of Kibbutz Nahalal near Tiberias. Left, one of the founders of the kibbutz, H. Bortniker

Gymnastic festival, 1913. Sephardi team entering the arena. Palestine was still Turkish – note the crescent inside the Zionist Star of David

Casino in Tel-Aviv in the 1930s

Above: Nahum Sokolow, one of the founding fathers of modern Israel, addresses a public meeting in
1920
Facing: Settlers celebrate the issuing of the Balfour Declaration in November 1917 and the advance
of the British troops in Palestine in 1918

Above: Before the Second World War there were five waves of immigration into Palestine. The first two, in the 1880s and in the decade up to 1914, brought settlers from Eastern Europe. These laid the foundations of the labour movement. The third and fourth waves brought many middle-class immigrants. The fifth, from 1929 to 1939, predominantly brought in Jews from Germany. This picture shows a young immigrant from Germany
Facing: After an Arab attack on Jewish settlers in Hebron, 1929

Above: Members of Kibbutz Massadah building defences against Arab attack, 1937
Below: Mounted Jewish self-defence force, 1936

Picture sources

Archiv Stümpfl, Vienna

55

Bildarchiv der Österr. Nationalbibliothek, Vienna

20/21, 24, 26/27, 28 (1), 30, 43, 48/49, 62, 68/69, 71 (1),
74/75, 83, 85 (2), 86 (2), 87, 88, 89 (2), 90, 91 (2), 92, 93, 95,
96, 97, 98 (3), 99 (1), 100 (1), 101, 102/103, 104, 106 (2), 107,
108 (2), 109, 110 (2), 112, 113, 118 (2), 119, 123, 124 (1), 125,
141, 154 (3), 155, 157 (1), 209, 212 (1), 216 (3), 217 (1)

Hilscher, Vienna

105

Österr. Filmmuseum, Vienna

196, 198, 199 (2), 200 (2), 201, 202, 203

Österr. Staatsarchiv/Kriegsarchiv, Vienna

29, 31, 50, 51, 54, 60, 61, 63, 64, 65, 66, 67, 77, 122 (1)

Stadtmuseum, Cracow

32

Prof. Skopeč, Prague

126, 127

Stadtarchiv, Prague

120/121, 124 (1), 128

Archives photographiques, Paris

131, 135, 136

Bibliothèque Nationale, Paris

130, 134, 138, 148, 156 (1)

Museé Nissim de Camondo, Paris

132 (3), 133

Annette Vaillant, Paris

138

Roger Violett, Paris

129, 137, 146 (2), 147, 149 (2)

Windsor Castle Library (Crown Copyright)

165

Mocatta Library, University College, London

150, 161 (1), 163

Radio Times Hulton Picture Library, London

152 (2), 153, 156 (1), 158 (3), 160 (1), 166/167, 169, 170, 171,
172, 173 (3), 174 (2), 175 (2)

Victoria and Albert Museum, London

162 (1), 164, 168

Wiener Library, London

227

S. Fischer-Verlag, Frankfurt

207

J. Hamann, Hamburg

222/223, 229, 230, 231

Staatsbibliothek Berlin, Bildarchiv

208 (1), 212 (2), 214, 217 (1)

Stadtmuseum, Frankfurt

151, 220

Ullstein-Bilderdienst, Berlin

140, 206, 208 (1), 215

Archives of Helena Rubinstein, New York

259

Bettmann Archives, New York

195, 245, 253 (2)

The Library of Congress, Washington

234 (1), 237, 238, 246 (1)

Culver Pictures, New York

232/233, 234 (1), 236, 241, 244, 251 (2), 254 (1), 262 (2), 264 (3), 265 (2), 268/269

Museum of the City of New York

197, 239, 240, 243, 246 (1), 247, 248, 249 (1), 250 (2), 251 (1), 252, 253 (1), 254 (1), 255 (1), 256, 257, 261, 263, 266, 267 (2), 270

The New York Public Library

235

Prof. Roman Vishniac (A. Kacyzna and R. Vishniac)

33, 34, 35, 36, 41, 45 (2), 46, 52, 53

Central Archives of the History of Jewish People, Jerusalem

44, 122 (1), 183 (1), 184, 185 (2)

Central Zionist Archives, Jerusalem

178, 179, 180, 181 (2), 182 (2), 273, 276 (2), 277, 278 (2), 279, 284–303, 307, 308, 310, 311, 312, 313, 315, 316

Yad Vashem, Jerusalem

23, 37 (1), 38 (1), 39, 40 (2), 42, 47, 50, 63

Keren Kayemeth, Jerusalem

304, 305, 306, 309, 314

The Jewish National and University Library

72, 73, 78, 100 (1), 111, 114, 115, 116, 117, 125 (1), 161 (1), 183 (1), 210 (1), 211, 218, 219, 249 (1), 258 (2), 260, 274, 275, 282, 283

Special thanks are due to Mr Moses Heiman Gans and Verlag Bosch und Keuning of Baarn, for allowing me to reproduce the plates on pages 186 – 94 from the splendid book, *Memorboek, platenatlas van het leven der joden in Nederland,* as well as to the Jewish Museum, London, for its special help and assistance. I also wish to thank Europa Verlag, Zürich, for the plate on page 145 from *W. Uhde, Von Bismarck bis Picasso* and Diogenes Verlag, Zürich for the plate on page 139 from *Walter Mehring, Verrufene Malerei.*

It is not possible to list all the very many people who gave me unstinting assistance in researching the material for this book. I would like to thank them all here and to crave their future support. Above all, I hope my work meets with their approval.

Franz Hubmann